PS WAVERLEY
THE FIRST SIXTY YEARS

PS WAVERLEY
THE FIRST SIXTY YEARS

ALISTAIR DEAYTON
AND IAIN QUINN

TEMPUS

Acknowledgements

The authors wish to thank Edward Quinn, Ian Somerville, Douglas McGowan, Richard Danielson, Peter Box, Chris Jones, Margaret Skee, the Clyde River Steamer Club and the Bute Museum for the use of photographs; also photographs by the late John Ramsay, Graham E. Langmuir and Hamish Stewart have been used. We would like to apologise for not acknowledging any photographs by any other photographer that may have made their way into the collections of the authors and been reproduced here.

The authors wish to accord their thanks to the masters, crew and directors of WSN and WEL over the years who have given steamer enthusiasts and the public an enormous amount of pleasure.

We would also like to thank the Clyde River Steamer Club, Paddle Steamer Preservation Society, West Highland Steamer Club and Coastal Cruising Association for stimulating interest in *Waverley* through the years.

Frontispiece: Waverley off Rothesay, Isle of Bute, in 1973.

First published 2007

Tempus Publishing
Cirencester Road, Chalford,
Stroud, Gloucestershire, GL6 8PE
www.tempus-publishing.com

Tempus Publishing is an imprint of NPI Media Group

© Alistair Deayton and Iain Quinn, 2007

The right of Alistair Deayton and Iain Quinn to be
identified as the Authors of this work has been asserted
in accordance with the Copyrights, Designs and Patents Act 1988.

British Library Cataloguing in Publication Data.
A catalogue record for this book is available from the British Library.

ISBN 978 0 7524 4473 4

Typesetting and origination by NPI Media Group
Printed in Great Britain

Contents

Foreword

It is hard to believe that the iconic paddle steamer *Waverley*, the grand old lady of the Clyde, celebrates her Diamond Jubilee in 2007. Who would have thought that back in 1974 – when a bunch of eager enthusiasts (including myself) from the Paddle Steamer Preservation Society purchased her for the famous fee of £1 from Caledonian MacBrayne Ltd – that she would still be giving pleasure to thousands, not just on the Firth of Clyde but all around the British coast, over thirty years on?

Her survival is no accident of fate. She proudly carries the title of 'last sea-going paddle steamer in the world' and, as such, deserves to have won her place in maritime history. Her survival is due in no small measure to the generosity of the Heritage Lottery Fund and other agencies, who contributed to the ship's major £7million rebuild at Great Yarmouth. Ironically, the ship is probably in better condition now than when she was built in 1947.

It is right and proper that we pause to celebrate the magnificent achievement which is *Waverley*'s survival into the twenty-first-century. Part of that celebration is this excellent photographic history by Iain Quinn and Alistair Deayton, which so beautifully illustrates the many ports, harbours and piers she has visited since 1947. I was aboard the *Waverley* when she first left the Clyde in April 1977 to 'test the market' in Liverpool and the River Mersey. It was an exciting and adventurous voyage and one which proved beyond all doubt that the old girl had thousands of admirers south of the border. Even then, we never dreamed that only two years later, she would settle into a routine which would take her yearly to the Western Isles and the Bristol Channel in the spring, followed by the Clyde for the main summer season, concluding with six weeks on the South Coast and Thames Estuary.

Iain and Alistair have painstakingly researched various sources to identify rare photographs of this fine ship in unusual nooks and crannies. Sometimes these calls by *Waverley* are one-off affairs, never to be repeated. Others are photographs of more familiar places where *Waverley* calls on a regular basis.

The challenges of keeping this twentieth-century dinosaur, with its magnificent triple-expansion steam engines, operating in a twenty-first century constantly changing Health and Safety regime are very real. But YOU can play YOUR part by coming aboard *Waverley* with your family and friends in this very special sixtieth year. You will be helping to keep *Waverley*'s paddles turning for future generations to enjoy!

DOUGLAS McGOWAN
Former Chairman: *Waverley* Excursions Ltd.
Honorary President: Paddle Steamer Preservation Society (Scottish Branch).

Introduction

2007 marks *Waverley*'s sixtieth year, a timespan only surpassed by two Clyde steamers, *Lucy Ashton* (1888-1949) and *Iona* (1864-1935), although *Duchess of Argyll* (1906-1970) and *Queen Mary II* (1933-date) have lasted longer with long spells in static use. *Glengarry* (1844-1927), *Premier* (1846-1937), *Mary Jane/Glencoe* (1846-1931) and *Chevalier* (1866-1927) all served for more than sixty years, but with only a handful of these years in Clyde service.

2007 also marks the thirtieth anniversary of *Waverley*'s first trip outside the Clyde, a weekend spent operating out of Liverpool. Every year since has seen her sailing for several weeks outwith the Firth of Clyde during which time she has called at around 200 piers and harbours, the majority of which are illustrated in this volume.

Waverley's history is well known: she was built in 1947 for the London & North Eastern Railway to replace the 1899 paddle steamer of the same name, which had been sunk at Dunkirk in 1940. In the following year when the railways were nationalised, she became part of the fleet of the Caledonian Steam Packet Co., which was merged with David MacBrayne Ltd to form Caledonian MacBrayne in 1973. She was withdrawn from service after the 1973 summer season, by which time she was the last sea-going paddle steamer in the world. In 1974, the Paddle Steamer Preservation Society purchased her for preservation for the symbolic sum of £1.

In 1975, against all the odds and contrary to the expectations of all but a handful of diehard enthusiasts, she started operating on the Clyde for the summer season. 1977 saw the aforementioned visits to Liverpool and a catastrophic grounding on the Gantocks Rocks off Dunoon. In 1978 she made her first visit to the Solent area and to the Thames Estuary and in 1979 to the Bristol Channel. These areas have all featured in her programme annually ever since.

1982 saw the first sailings out of Oban, which now form an eagerly awaited start to her season in early May each year. Other areas of the United Kingdom have seen occasional calls, including the East Coast of England; the Forth and the Tay in 1981 and 1982; the Republic of Ireland in 1985, 1986 and 1990; in 1986, Stornoway and Tarbert; Harris in 1989 and 1990, and Castlebay, Barra and Lochboisdale, South Uist, in 1990.

Throughout the period of her preservation, she has made occasional calls at closed piers in the Firth of Clyde and in recent years *Waverley* has seen the rebuilding and reopening of piers at Lochranza and Blairmore – which again see regular calls – also, beyond the Clyde, piers at Southwold and Newport have been rebuilt, as have those at Penarth, Clevedon and Ilfracombe.

Over the 1999-2000 winter *Waverley* underwent an extensive £3 million rebuild, financed by the Heritage Lottery Fund, which covered the hull, engines and the aft-passenger accommodation. Over the 2002/03 winter the forward-passenger accommodation was rebuilt and this was also funded by the Heritage Lottery Fund.

Over her sixty-year career, and particularly over her thirty years in preservation, *Waverley* has earned a very special place in the affections of both steamer enthusiasts and the general public. Long may she continue to sail. Her continued sailing relies, of course, on you, your friends and your family sailing on her and not just looking at the pictures in this book.

Waverley Timeline: Appearance

1947: Built for the London & North Eastern Railway to replace *Waverley* of 1899 which had been sunk at Dunkirk in 1940. Appearance as today, except she had canvas dodgers on the bridge wings, windows rather than portholes in the sponsons, no emergency exit from the dining room on the aft promenade deck. The starboard fore lifeboat and the two aft lifeboats are no longer there.

1 January 1948: With the nationalisation of the railways, *Waverley* was now owned by the British Transport Commission, although she operated as part of the Caledonian Steam Packet fleet. Her funnels were repainted yellow with a black top before the beginning of the summer season.

1952: Ownership transferred to the Caledonian Steam Packet Co. Ltd (CSP).

1953: Deckhouses, which had been painted in scumbled (wood-effect) brown, were repainted in white. This was the last year with two gold lines on her hull.

1956-1957: During the winter months, *Waverley* was converted from coal to oil firing.

1959: The paddle boxes were painted white.

1961: The forward funnel was renewed. This was not quite aligned with the aft funnel and she sailed like this until the rebuild in 2000.

1962: After funnel was renewed, *Waverley*'s last refit at A. & J. Inglis of Glasgow.

1965: With the advent of British Rail's corporate image, *Waverley* was repainted in common with the remainder of the CSP fleet, with a Monastral Blue hull and red metal lions rampant added to the funnels.

1969: The CSP became part of the Scottish Transport Group and were no longer under railway control. *Waverley*'s masts were shortened to fit under the new Kingston Bridge, although she never actually went under.

1970: The hull was repainted black. With the withdrawal of *Caledonia* after the previous season she was now the sole steamer sailing from Craigendoran. Following the withdrawal of *Caledonia* and *Ryde* she was now the last sea-going paddle steamer in the world.

1971: From July to the end of the season *Waverley* sailed with a stump foremast after being blown against Arrochar Pier and snapping the mast.

1972: Her paddle boxes were repainted in black with white edges and a new foremast was fitted.

1973: The CSP became part of Caledonian MacBrayne Ltd. Therefore, her funnels were painted in their house colours of red with a yellow circle encompassing the lions – this was done after a couple of days with an unsuccessful experimental livery of red with a yellow band and black top.

8 August 1974: Sold to *Waverley* Steam Navigation Company (WSN) for preservation for a symbolic sum of £1.

1975: Funnels repainted in the LNER red, white and black colours.

1976: Lifeboat covers red. From July only had three lifeboats.

1977: Paddle boxes reverted to all black for her thirtieth anniversary season.

1978: To allow visits to London, windows in sponsons replaced with portholes.

1980: Forward-funnel cowl vents removed, not replaced until heritage rebuild.

March 1981: New Babcock Steambloc boiler fitted to replace the original.

1983: Number of lifeboats reduced to two.

1984: WSN house flag affixed to spurkit plate on bow for this season only.

1985: Wooden wheelhouse replaced by an aluminium one.

1990: New paddle wheels complete.

1995: New after mast installed, made by Nobles of Girvan at a cost of £6,000. First application to Lottery submitted.

16 June 1997: In time for Golden Jubilee, Heritage Lottery money was awarded to the WSN project.

December 1999 to July 2000: Major £3 million rebuild at the yard of George Prior, Great Yarmouth, funded by the Heritage Lottery Fund. Her decks and deckhouses were removed, central and aft portions of the hull completely stripped and the engines dismantled and rebuilt. A new boiler was fitted and a new emergency exit from the dining salon to the aft deck constructed. The deckhouses were repainted in scumbled wood-effect finish, in a complete return to her LNER colours.

14 October 2002 to 11 June 2003: Second stage of rebuild, where her forward accommodation was rebuilt and the forward deck shelter and foremast replaced. With the exception of the new emergency exit from the dining saloon, the portholes replacing windows in the sponsons and the addition of a disabled toilet in the forward observation lounge, *Waverley* has been returned to her original 1947 appearance with exemplary attention to detail.

Waverley Timeline: Routes Served

16 June 1947: Entered service on the route from Craigendoran and Rothesay to Lochgoilhead and Arrochar, the regular route in her early years. From early May to the beginning of the summer season from 1947 until 1953 she was also on the Craigendoran to Rothesay service.

18 February to 29 March 1949: First spell in winter service, relieving *Talisman* for overhaul with sailings from Craigendoran to Gourock and an occasional trip to Rothesay.

13 January to 1 April 1950: Operated on the winter service from Craigendoran to Rothesay.

1952: *Waverley* now sailed to Arrochar on Tuesdays, Thursdays and Saturdays, and round Bute on Mondays, Wednesdays and Fridays. During December *Waverley* operated the Gourock to Dunoon winter service until 4 March 1953, which she also did from October 1953 to 4 January 1954.

1953: Sailed to Arrochar on Tuesdays, Wednesdays and Thursdays; to Arran via the Kyles of Bute on Mondays and on a non-landing afternoon cruise to Brodick Bay on Fridays. This was augmented by railway connection work between Craigendoran, Gourock, Dunoon and Rothesay on Saturdays. A trip to Tighnabruaich was offered on Sundays.

4 January 1954: Final day of scheduled winter service, replaced by the car ferry *Arran* on the Gourock to Dunoon service at 12:20. Performed relief sailings on Fridays during the summer.

1955: A round-the-Lochs cruise replaced the Arrochar sailings on Wednesdays.

1958: An upriver cruise from the Clyde resorts to Glasgow (Bridge Wharf) was now offered on Fridays. Saturday sailings were almost entirely between Wemyss Bay and Rothesay. From now until 1962 *Waverley* replaced *Duchess of Hamilton* on the long-distance excursions to Inveraray and Campbeltown in September.

1961: *Waverley* alternated rosters with *Jeanie Deans*, so that in alternate weeks she had an afternoon cruise from Monday to Friday round Bute and a Saturday afternoon sailing to Tighnabruaich.

1963 and 1964: Replaced *Queen Mary II* on the Glasgow to Tighnabruaich service in September.

1965: Following the replacement of *Jeanie Deans* by *Caledonia*, *Waverley* continued the mix of cruise sailings as before, but with a round-Bute cruise on Mondays. Saturday sailings changed back to Craigendoran to Rothesay. She was used on a Sunday cruise to Skipness or round Bute on alternate Sundays. Lochgoilhead Pier closed in July and the call there was substituted by a Loch Goil cruise.

1967: Replaced *Talisman* on the Sunday afternoon cruises from Millport and Largs to Rothesay and Tighnabruaich.

1970: With the withdrawal of *Caledonia* after the previous season she was now the sole paddle steamer sailing from Craigendoran. Started a sailing to Tarbert and Ardrishaig on Fridays.

1971: Now based at Gourock as the Clyde excursion programme contracted. Still sailed on much the same trips: to Arran via the Kyles on Mondays; to Arrochar on Tuesdays from Rothesay; on Thursdays to Arrochar from Largs; round-the-Lochs trips on Wednesdays now incorporating an afternoon cruise round Bute; to Tarbert and Ardrishaig on Fridays and round Bute on Sundays. Keppel Pier (Millport) closed after this season.

1972: Waverley now performed a round-Bute cruise on Mondays, an additional round-the-Lochs sailing on Tuesdays and no longer called at Ardrishaig on Fridays. This year saw the last calls at Craigendoran and Arrochar.

1973: Thursday sailing was now round Bute. Withdrawn from service after the end of the season.

22 May 1975: Re-entered service, sailing at weekends from Glasgow (Anderston Quay) and in mid-week from Ayr. The Tuesday sailing from Ayr to Tarbert, Loch Fyne, has endured in the timetable to the present day.

May 1977: *Waverley*'s first sailings away from the Clyde, when she offered a week's sailing out of Liverpool to Llandudno and other destinations.

15 July 1977: *Waverley* ran aground on the Gantocks Rocks off Dunoon. Was off service for six weeks for hull repairs.

April to May 1978: First sailings on the Solent and the Thames. They have been offered every season since, more recently in September. The Glasgow berth was moved from Anderston Quay to Stobcross Quay.

1979: Regular calls at Helensburgh instituted during the Clyde season. Made one-off calls at Kilmun and Ardyne on a PSPS charter. This year saw *Waverley*'s first sailings on the Bristol Channel.

April to June 1981: Circumnavigated the British Isles for the first time, offering cruises on the Rivers Humber, Tyne and Forth. These were only offered in this and the following year.

1982: First sailings from Oban at the beginning of May, which are now a regular feature of the *Waverley* schedule. Also offered a weekend's sailings from Dundee.

13 April 1985: Sailed from Garlieston to Douglas, Isle of Man. *Waverley* made her first cruises from Dublin and other ports in the Republic of Ireland. These excursions were also offered in 1986 and in 1990. Sailings to the Isle of Man from the United Kingdom mainland do not feature in her current passenger certificates.

1988: Trips from Kyle of Lochalsh and Portree were added to the West Highland sailings.

1989: Sailings made from Tarbert, Harris and Stornoway, which were also offered in 1990, but she has not called there since. A sailing was offered from Castlebay, Barra and Lochboisdale, South Uist. These sailings from the Outer Hebrides were not repeated.

September 1992: *Waverley* made a one-off call at Carradale.

1993: Made a one-off call at Otter Ferry during Easter.

1994: Called at the Admiralty Pier at the former torpedo-testing station at Succoth, across Loch Long from Arrochar.

1995: Made a one-off call at Portencross.

19 August 2000: First sailing after the Heritage Lottery Fund rebuild.

29 June 2003: Lochranza Pier re-opened. This has become a regular call on her Sunday sailings.

2004: The Glasgow berth moved to the Science Centre, on the south bank of the river because of a new bridge being built at Finnieston, and because there was a lack of water at Anderston Quay at very low tides due to a lack of dredging in the upper river.

22 May 2005: Blairmore Pier re-opened. This has become a regular call on the Wednesday sailing to Loch Goil.

6: *Waverley* undertook special sailings to commemorate the sixtieth anniversary of her launch, with a cruise to Loch Long and Loch Goil on Saturday 14 October and to Tighnabruaich on Sunday 15, both from Glasgow.

8 and 12 May 2007: *Waverley* made her first calls at Inverie (Loch Nevis) and Colonsay, believed to be the first ever call by a paddle steamer at these places.

16 June 2007: Sixtieth anniversary of Maiden Voyage from Glasgow to Arrochar.

19 July 2007: Caledonian MacBrayne presented a brass plaque for the steamer's sixtieth anniversary.

Normally – although not every year – *Waverley* starts her programme with a weekend on the Clyde at Easter, followed by sailings from Oban on the Bank Holiday weekend at the beginning of May, extended in some seasons with a visit to Skye during the following week and a second weekend sailing out of Oban. The remainder of May sees special sailings and charters on the Clyde; June sees her sailing on the Bristol Channel; July and August on the Clyde and in September she sails on the Solent for the first couple of weeks or so, then moves to the Thames until the second weekend in October, where – in some seasons – the season closes with a weekend of Bristol Channel sailings. However, in 2006 and 2007 the season has closed with the sixtieth-anniversary sailings on the Clyde.

Her Clyde schedule is fairly constant:

Sundays: Glasgow at 10:00, Greenock and Largs to Lochranza via the Kyles of Bute and a cruise to Skipness from Lochranza.
Mondays: Glasgow at 10:00, and Large to Ayr, Girvan and round Ailsa Craig, with passenger returning to Glasgow, Largs and Girvan from Ayr by bus.
Tuesdays: Ayr at 10:00, Millport and Largs to Rothesay, Tighnabruaich and Tarbert and a cruise on Loch Fyne.
Wednesdays: Ayr at 10:00, Brodick and Largs to Dunoon, Blairmore, and a cruise on Loch Goil.
Thursdays: Greenock at 10:30 and Helensburgh, Dunoon, Rothesay and Largs to Millport, Brodick and a cruise round Holy Isle to Pladda.
Fridays: Glasgow at 10:00 and Kilcreggan to Dunoon and Rothesay, with an occasional evening cruise from Glasgow at 19:30.
Saturdays: Glasgow at 10:00, Greenock, and Helensburgh to Dunoon, Rothesay and Tighnabruaich.

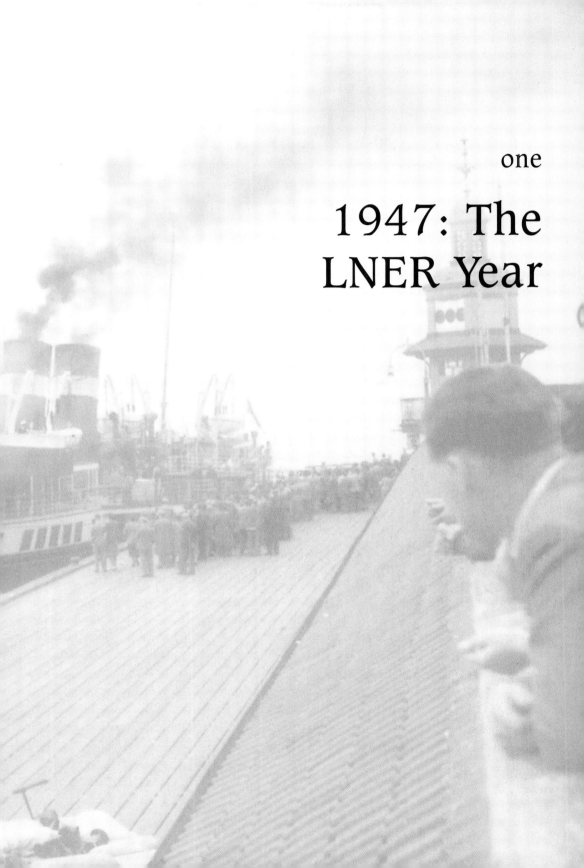

one

1947: The LNER Year

The present *Waverley* was built to replace the previous *Waverley* of 1899, which had been sunk at Dunkirk. In fact the plans for her were drawn up in 1938, and the LNER laid the 1899 steamer up in 1939, and would obviously have withdrawn her had the new steamer been built then, but war intervened. The 1899 *Waverley* is seen here in her 1936-38 colours approaching Dunoon.

The *Jeanie Deans'* post-war rebuild at A. & J. Inglis in 1946 was the obvious use of the drawings for the new steamer. *Jeanie Deans* is seen here in her 1946-47 condition.

Right: Waverley's keel was laid on 27 December 1945 and she is seen here, shortly after with the hull frames still to be fitted

Below: The frames whilst building the beginning of the framework that the hull plates would be riveted to. Note the rivet holes and compare with the illustrations on page 119.

Looking forward, showing the keel and hull frames.

The main deck is now being prepared, and the starboard paddle box drum has been fitted.

By now, the promenade deck has been planked and the forward companionway housing fitted.

A view across the River Kelvin on launch day, 2 October 1946.

Waverley is launched and heads down the slipway, viewed by the assembled crowd of dignitaries on the launch platform.

Launched, and dressed overall.

Fitting out in the River Kelvin, with DEPV *Talisman* on the slipway for overhaul behind her.

On 20 January 1947, *Waverley* was towed downriver to Victoria Harbour, Greenock, where she is seen here, for the fitting of her engines and boilers, manufactured by Rankin & Blackmore of Greenock.

Above: At Victoria Harbour, by now with her funnels fitted and turned round to enable the fitting of her port paddle wheel.

Left: On the afternoon of 16 June 1947, her first day in service, with the fan boards reading: 'Kirn, Dunoon, Innellan and Rothesay'. This photograph was taken after she had returned from her maiden voyage to Lochgoilhead and Arrochar.

Opposite above: Going astern out of Arrochar on 16 June 1947, her first day in service.

Opposite below: At Dunoon in 1947, with the stern of *Jeanie Deans* to be seen.

At Bowling in the winter of 1947/48, with both funnels now in British Railway colours and *Lucy Ashton* laid up alongside her.

Waverley spent the winter of 1947/48 laid up in Bowling Harbour, where her funnels are seen in the process of being repainted into British Railway's yellow and black livery.

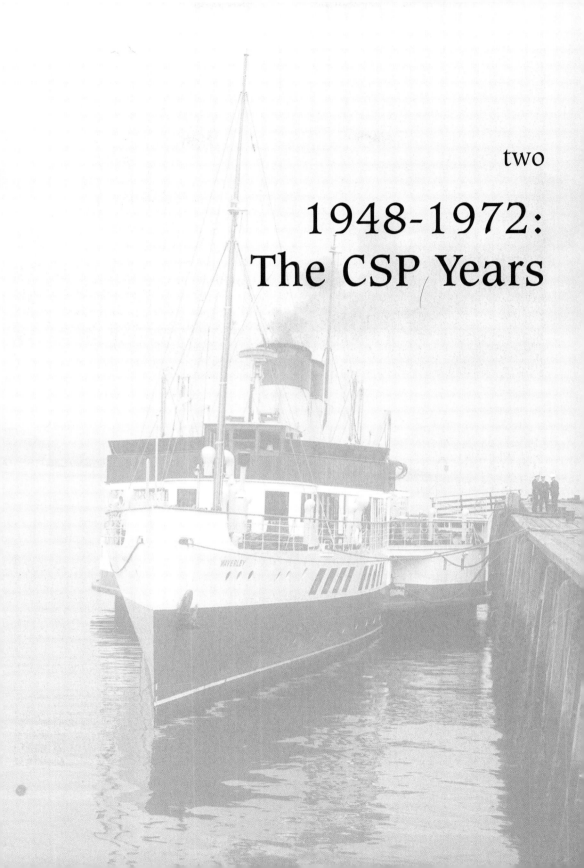

two

1948-1972:
The CSP Years

Left: After the closure of Bridge Wharf in 1971, *Waverley* made occasional charter trips from Glasgow's Princes Dock, where she is seen here.

Below: Heading downriver off Renfrew Ferry in 1953.

Above: Passing Yoker Power Station in 1953.

Below: Waverley with *Caledonia* and one of the *Maids* at her home port of Craigendoran, taken from the West Highland Railway.

Arriving at Lochgoilhead in the early 1950s.

Waverley at her original destination, Arrochar, in her 1959–1960 condition with lions on the funnels and the monastral blue hull. She has built for the Craigendoran to Lochgoilhead and Arrochar service, but was moved to a more varied selection of routes from 1952 onwards.

In the winter of 1967/68 she was laid up alongside *Queen Mary II* in Queen's Dock.

Juxtaposition of funnels, with *Queen Mary II* in Queen's Dock, 1967/68.

Heading upriver, about to pass a Blue Star liner, in her 1959/60 condition with her original funnels.

1969/70 saw her laid up for the winter in Rothesay Dock alongside the recently withdrawn *Caledonia*.

A deck view in Rothesay Dock with *Caledonia*, 1969/70.

Waverley, unusually in James Watt Dock in Greenock, in the autumn of 1970, laid up for the winter.

Waverley laid up alongside the recently withdrawn *Jeanie Deans* in Greenock Albert Harbour in the winter of 1964/65.

Waverley at Gourock at low tide in 1969.

At Craigendoran, awaiting passengers in the late 1960s.

Arriving at Gourock in the 1950s.

Approaching Gourock in 1971.

Waverley approaching Largs in 1970 or 1971.

Departing Innellan in the late 1960s.

At Rothesay in the late 1960s. Rather unusually, *Waverley* is seen with her anchor out.

Waverley at Lochranza, Isle of Arran, on the occasion of a Clyde River Steamer Club charter, in 1971.

At Whiting Bay, Isle of Arran, the longest pier on the Clyde, on 19 July 1954.

Dressed overall at Tarbert, Loch Fyne, on the occasion of a Clyde River Steamer Club charter in April 1966.

Off Gourock in 1968, with Loch Long in the background.

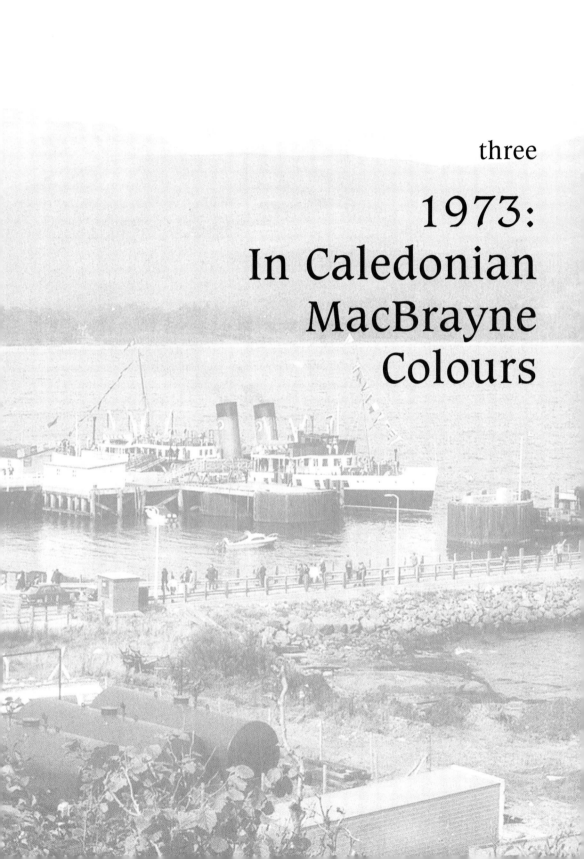

three

1973:
In Caledonian
MacBrayne
Colours

At Gourock in 1973.

Approaching Dunoon in her 1973 condition with CalMac funnels and black paddle boxes.

Waverley arriving at Millport, Isle of Cumbrae, in the 1973 season.

At Brodick, Isle of Arran, on 11 September 1973. Note the then new linkspan with its approach road and Arran's highest mountain, Goatfell (2,866ft).

Waverley approaching Wemyss Bay on the River Clyde dressed overall in flags and in CalMac colours in 1973. (J. & C. McCutcheon)

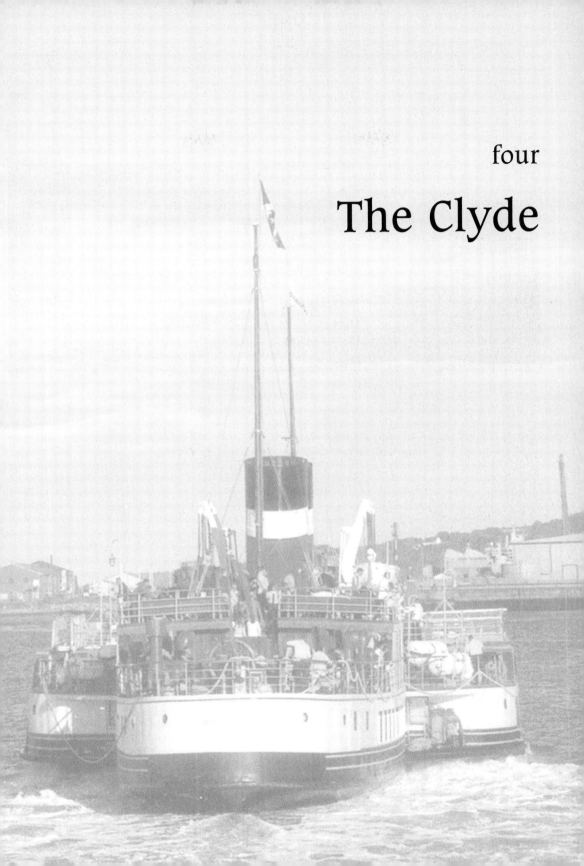

four

The Clyde

Above: Raising steam for the first time under Waverley Steam Navigation ownership, 14 May 1975.

Left: Waverley at her berth at Anderston Quay with the cranes of the now demolished General Terminus ore terminal still visible on the south bank.

Opposite above: At Anderston Quay from the south bank, with *Balmoral* hiding behind her.

Opposite below: Waverley at Stobcross Quay in Spring 1981, when her boiler was being replaced, with her funnels on the quayside.

At her short-lived Glasgow mooring at Stobcross Quay, used from 1978 to 1983.

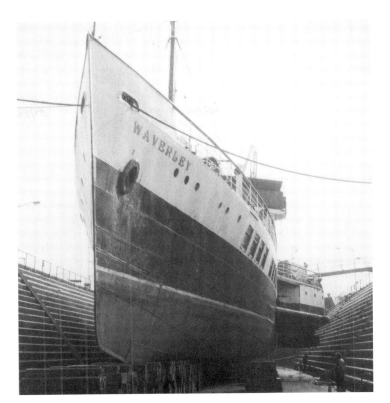

Right: In Govan Dry Dock for her winter overhaul, April 1980.

Below: Passing the Glasgow Garden Festival in 1988.

Heading back upriver, leaving John Brown's shipyard after calling there on a charter.

Heading downriver off Renfrew, from an aircraft arriving at Glasgow Airport, 13 May 1986, with the Isle of Wight ferry *Freshwater* being transformed into Western Ferries *Sound of Seil* in the background. (Richard Danielson)

Sailing back to Glasgow from Greenock.

Waverley rendezvousing with Cunard's *Queen Elizabeth 2*, on the latter's first return to the Clyde since her building, 1990.

In 1999, during the Tall Ships Race at Greenock, she berthed at the entrance to the Victoria Harbour instead of her usual berth at Custom House Quay. Note the pilot cutter *Clyde* in the basin.

Waverley at Greenock Custom House Quay with the preservved cargo steamer *Shieldhall* on 28 July 2005. *Shieldhall* was built in 1955 as a sludge steamer for Glasgow Corporation, taking treated sewage from Shieldhall or Dalmuir Sewage Works to the dumping grounds off Garroch Head. In 1977 she was sold for use at Southampton, and has been preserved there since 1988, offering occasional public passenger trips. In 2005 she visited the Clyde for her Golden Jubilee.

Berthing at Gourock, from the linkspan.

Off Cumbrae, greeting preserved steamer *Shieldhall* in the customary way with a blast of the whistle, 2005.

Waverley, unusually, moored along the south side of Largs Pier, normally only used in adverse weather conditions.

At Millport in her first season under preservation in 1975.

In 1977, following the grounding of *Waverley* on the Gantocks, the motor vessel *Queen of Scots* was chartered to maintain services whilst *Waverley* was undergoing hull repairs. Both vessels are seen here at Millport on 1 September of that year, *Queen of Scots* having just transferred stores to *Waverley*. (Walter Kerr)

Moored at the former Admiralty torpedo-testing station pier at Succoth, across Loch Long from Arrochar, in 1997. It appears that one of the authors is seriously bothered by midges!

Opposite above: In September 1977 *Waverley* made a special call at Kilmun, where Western Ferries' *Sound of Sanda*, ex-*Lymington*, berthed outside her.

Opposite below: Unusually berthed along the west side of Helensburgh Pier. Shallow water means *Waverley* can only berth here at high tide.

Moored at the new Dunoon Pier/breakwater, 25 August 2005.

Opposite above: On 15 September 1979, whilst on a PSPS charter, she called at the pier at Ardyne, the site of a short-lived oil rig construction yard.

Opposite below: Berthed unusually across the west end of Rothesay Pier.

Above: In the early part of the Summer 2007 season, *Waverley* berthed across the west end of Rothesay Pier because of building work taking place on the pier for a new car ferry berth. She is seen here on 15 June 2007.

Left: Waverley across the west end of Rothesay Pier, taken from the Albert Pier, 22 June 2007.

At a one-off call at Otter Ferry, Easter 1993. The pier here could only be used after Captain Steve Michel had repaired it with planks he had supplied himself.

Heading up the Kyles of Bute towards Colintraive, 1995.

Approaching Lochranza, Isle of Arran.

Opposite above: At Inveraray at the head of Loch Fyne during her second season in preservation, 1976.

Opposite below: On the same occasion at Inveraray, taken from the Bell Tower.

Above: Going astern out of Brodick, 1987.

Left: Approaching her regular Monday destination of Ailsa Craig, 1977.

Full astern away from Troon, 1995.

Above: Waverley has made an occasional special sailing to Stranraer at the head of Loch Ryan, where she is seen here on 16 May 1986 with the Sealink ferry *Darnia*. (Richard Danielson)

Left: 1977 saw a special sailing to Cairnyan in Loch Ryan, where she is seen here.

This sailing continued down the Galloway coast to off Portpatrick, further south than any previous Clyde steamer had ever operated in scheduled passenger-carrying service.

Occasional sailings have operated to Red Bay on the Antrim coast from Ayr and Campbeltown.

Heading north from Dunoon.

1. *Waverley* saw occasional service from Glasgow Bridge Wharf, where she is seen here in September 1968. This was mainly on the Friday upriver run from Largs, Rothesay and Dunoon, but also for charters. In 2007 Bridge Wharf was totally removed to facilitate a new bridge.

2. *(Overleaf)* Funnels and paddle-box in 1970 or 1971, departing Rothesay for Tighnabruiach.

3. *Waverley* at Tighnabruiach in pre-1964 colours.

4. *Waverley* at Ardrishaig in 1970 or 1971, when a Friday Ardrishaig sailing replaced the upriver trips.

5. A stern view leaving Rothesay in 1970 or 1971.

6. On a one-off special call at the private pier at Portencross, Easter Sunday, 1995, the first call there by a Clyde steamer since 1914.

7. At Portencross, with the mountains of Arran shrouded in mist in the background.

8. Arriving at Tarbert shortly after her re-entry into service after her rebuild. This photograph was taken in 2000.

9. At Ardrishaig Pier on a CRSC charter, with a preserved MacBrayne's bus in 1996.

10. Lochranza has been a regular Sunday call since the re-opening of the pier on 29 June 2003.

11. In Lamlash bay on a PSPS charter, September 1978. Passengers disembarked by means of the small boat *Mulloch Mhor*, from which this photograph was taken.

12. In Govan Dry Dock, covered in snow, April 1980.

13. At Oban North Pier in 1999 showing the Hutcheson Memorial on Kerrera, commemorating the pioneer steamer operator in the West Highlands and Islands and the old North Pier buildings which were removed in 2000.

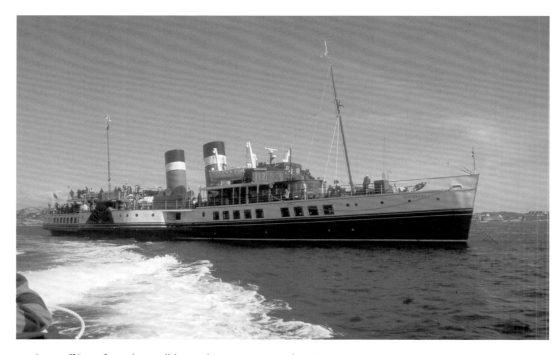

14. Seen off Iona from the small boat taking passengers ashore in 2001.

15. At anchor in the Sound of Iona, showing the coast of Mull in the background.

16. Her first visit to Colonsay on 12 May 2007, believed to be the first ever call by any paddle steamer at the island.

17. In dry dock at Birkenhead following an incident off Sanda in 2004. The MCA insisted on a dry-docking check to make sure that the hull had not been damaged.

18. At Douglas Victoria Pier at low tide, taken from the IOMSP's *King Orry*. (Richard Danielson)

19. *Waverley* sailed from Republic of Ireland ports in 1985, 1986 and 1990. She is seen here at Wicklow.

20. *Waverley* at Dundalk.

21. Passing Newport Transporter Bridge on 1 June 2007. (Chris Jones)

Opposite: 22. Moored at Cardiff, Roath Basin, May 2007. (Chris Jones)

23. Arriving at the Britannia Quay, Roath Basin, Cardiff on May 2007. (Chris Jones)

24. The island of Lundy has long been a favourite destination for Bristol Channel excursion steamers, and landing was by small boat until the pier, seen here, was built in 2001.

25. *Waverley* at Bournemouth, seen from the beach, in 1982.

26. Departing from Poole Quay in 1986.

27. The 2002/03 winter saw the second stage of the rebuild at Colin Prior's yard at Great Yarmouth and *Waverley* is seen here on the pontoon prior to it being pumped out and lifted to enable work to be done below the waterline. Work had already started to remove the windows in the Jeanie Deans Lounge and to remove the forward deck saloon. (Peter Box)

28. *Waverley* on the pontoon at Prior's yard.

five

The West Highlands

Approaching Oban Railway Pier, 1984.

Opposite above: On her annual visits to Oban and the West Highlands, *Waverley* normally makes a call on the way up at Port Ellen, Islay.

Opposite below: Waverley at Oban North Pier.

Silhouetted by the sunset at Oban North Pier, 2002.

Night at Oban North Pier, 1982.

Berthed at Craignure, Isle of Mull, with *Glen Sannox* and a model of *Waverley* in the foreground.

At Fort William during 2006.

Heading up Loch Linnhe with Ben Nevis in the background, 2001.

Anchored in the Sound of Iona, post-rebuild, with the coast of Mull behind her.

Waverley on her first visit to Crinan on 3 May 1985.

Opposite above: Anchored off Iona, with *Lochbuie* arriving and one of the small vessels tendering to *Waverley* just leaving the slip.

Opposite below: At Tobermory, Isle of Mull, with a rainbow.

At Coll in 2002, on the first visit there by a paddle steamer since *Pioneer* in 1942.

Opposite above: A deck shot at Coll in 2002.

Opposite below: At the Admiralty Pier at Mallaig, her only call there, on her first visit in 1988.

Left: Fanboards for her first cruise from Mallaig to Kyle of Lochalsh, in 1988.

Below: At the pier on the island of Raasay.

Above: On 10 May 2007, *Waverley* made her inaugural call at the new pier at Inverie on Loch Nevis. This is noteworthy as being he most isolated pier in Britain, as there is no road access. The pub in the village is famous for being the most isolated pub in Britian.

Below: Inverie is normally served from Mallaig by the small motor vessel *Western Isles*, seen along the side of the pier on 10 May, whilst *Waverley* is berthed across the end of the pier in magnificent surroundings.

Arriving at Tarbert, Harris.

Opposite above: At Broadford, Isle of Skye, in May 1995, the first call here by any steamer since *Fusilier* in 1933.

Opposite below: Departing Dunvegan, Skye, on 25 April 1995.

At Tarbert, Harris.

At Stornoway, Admiralty Pier, which she visited in 1989 and 1990.

Departing Stornoway.

Berthed at the MacBrayne Pier at Stornoway.

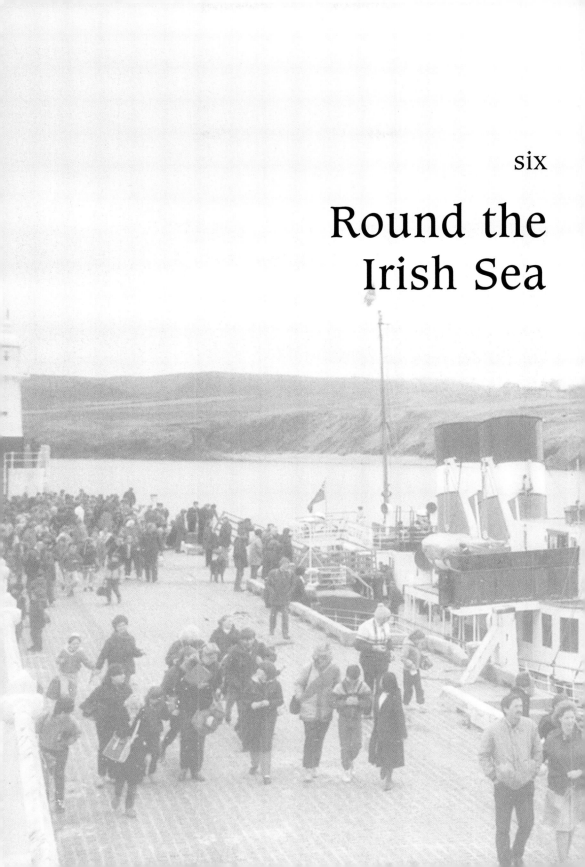

six

Round the
Irish Sea

Arriving at Llandudno on the first cruise from Liverpool on 1 May 1977.

Opposite: above: Waverley seen here on Sunday 1 May 1977, made her first trip outside the Clyde from Liverpool on a trip to Llandudno and a cruise off Anglesey.

Opposite below: Waverley with a full complement of daytrippers aboard leaving Fleetwood, *c.*1980. (J. & C. McCutcheon)

Arrived back at Liverpool, at the old Landing Stage, with the Liver buildings in the background.

Passing Cammell Laird's yard at Birkenhead in June 2001.

Waverley has visited Douglas, Isle of Man, where she is seen here, on various occasions since April 1985.

Waverley berthed at Peel, Isle of Man.

Waverley at Douglas in 1986, with the Isle of Man Steam Packet's *Mona's Queen*. (Richard Danielson)

Stormbound at Peel, 18 May 1986. Waverley Excursions have to be very imaginative at times when weather prevents the proposed cruise, and arrangements have to be made to call at alternative ports. They often have to arrange bus transport at short notice to return passengers to their starting point. (Richard Danielson)

Passengers disembarking at Peel on 30 April 1985. (Richard Danielson)

Waverley has on occasion offered sailings to and from Northern Ireland ports, although in recent years these have been undertaken by her fleet-mate *Balmoral*. She is seen here at Warrenpoint on 20 May 1991.

Waverley at Donagahadee, also in May 1991.

Waverley at Arklow.

In 1986 she sailed round to the Cork area, and is seen here at Cobh.

A sailing was made up the River Barrow to New Ross, where she is seen here passing through the railway swing bridge.

Waverley at Cork Anderson's Quay in 1985.

seven

The Bristol
Channel

The Bristol Channel has been a destination of choice for *Waverley* since her first visit there in 1979, and she is seen here sailing down the Avon, passing under the Clifton Suspension Bridge in 1988. Both authors hope that trips up the Avon can be restored to her timetable at some time in the future.

Arriving at Bristol, inside the Floating Harbour, passing Brunel's preserved pioneer liner *Great Britain*.

Heading up the River Usk under the transporter bridge in Newport on 1 June 2007. (Chris Jones)

Moored at the newly restored Church Street Wharf at Newport on 1 June 2007.

Waverley at Cardiff on her first visit to the docks, for refuelling, in 2006.

At a deserted quayside in Barry, where the first thoughts of preserving *Waveley* were mooted by Mr Terry Sylvester in 1974.

Waverley, off Barry, showing the old dock building in the background to the right, during May 2007. (Chris Jones)

Arriving at Tenby, one of the more unusual Bristol Channel ports of call.

Waverley berthed at Tenby.

Above: 'Three Ships Day' at Lundy with *Balmoral* and *Oldenburg*, on 18 June 1986, the occasion of their first meeting

Below:Waverley at Ilfracombe in 1979, along with *Balmoral*, then still operated by P. & A. Campbell.

In 1979, storms around Land's End forced her to put into St Ives for shelter on a positioning voyage from the Clyde to the South Coast. Note the main deck windows all have storm boards fitted for the voyage round Lands End. (L. Bennetts)

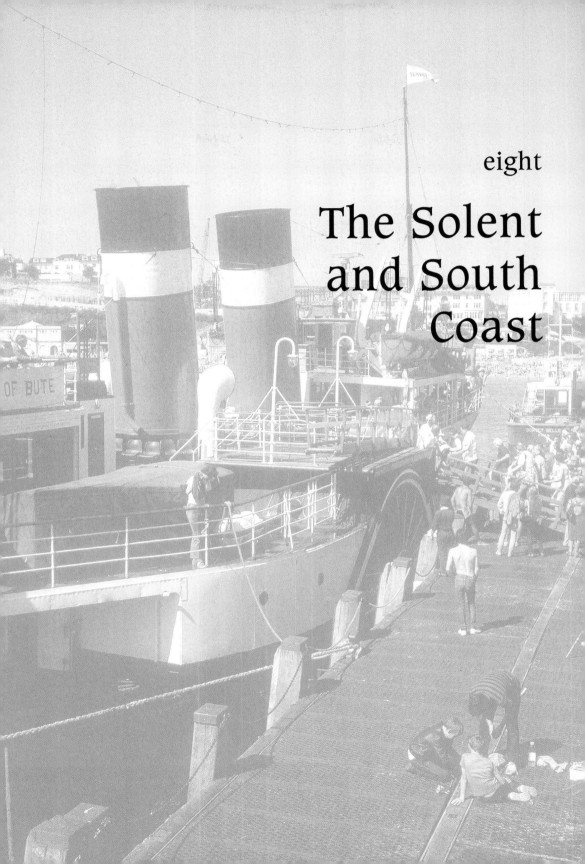

eight

The Solent and South Coast

Waverley at Torquay on her only visit there in 1979.

Opposite above: Waverley has made the very occasional trip from Falmouth, where she is seen here in 1984. (Richard Danielson)

Opposite below: Occasional sailings have also been offered from Kingswear on the River Dart, as on this occasion on 18 May 1998. (Richard Danielson)

Overleaf: The Solent and Dorset coast areas have long been popular for paddle steamer excursion. She is seen here at Bournemouth Pier in 1982.

Moored at Swanage. Due to health and safety concerns, the pier at Swanage has been unable to be used by *Waverley* since 2005.

Unlike the Cosen's steamers of old, *Waverley* did not run herself ashore at Lulworth Cove to land passengers, but merely cruises off it. Here she is seen in a 1982 cruise to the Jurassic Coast.

At Weymouth in 1979, with Sealink's *Earl Godwin* arriving.

At Yarmouth, Isle of Wight, with the Lymington ferry behind her and *Balmoral* at the pier head.

At Southampton (Town Quay), with a Red Funnel catamaran arriving and a Red Funnel car ferry on her way down Southampton Water.

At Southampton Town Quay, with *QE2* in the background, September 1986.

Arriving at Portsmouth's Clarence Pier in 1982.

On her first call at Southampton Royal Pier in 1978.

Waverley steaming into the famous dockyard at Portsmouth.

At Ryde Pier, seen from behind the Esplanade station, 1982.

At Newhaven with the Sealink ferry *Valencay*.

nine

The Thames Estuary and the East Coast of England

A highlight of the Thames sailings is the sailing through Tower Bridge, as seen here in 1979.

At Tower Pier, from Tower Bridge, in 1979.

A tug is required to turn *Waverley* in the pool of London, where she is seen here, turning off HMS *Belfast*.

At Tilbury, from the Gravesend ferry, in 2005.

Moored at Chatham Historic Dockyard, home of PS *Kingswear Castle*.

At Whitstable, with PS *Kingswear Castle*, 1986.

2 October 2002 saw the re-opening of Southwold Pier by *Waverley*. (Peter Box)

During the first stage of the rebuild in 1999/2000 – at George Prior's yard at Great Yarmouth – the funnels were replaced.

The boilers were also replaced; this photograph shows one of the new boilers manufactured by Cochran of Annan being lowered into position.

Also replaced was the hull plating below the boilers.

An interior view of the new hull plates.

Above: During the rebuild, the after deck shelter was replaced.

Left: The engines and crankshaft were totally overhauled.

The paddle wheels also received a total overhaul.

New sponsons were manufactured for the *Waverley* rebuild at Prior's yard on the Humber.

This photograph shows how the new sponsons looked when fitted.

With the hull in a grey undercoat and the funnels not yet painted, *Waverley* presented a new colour scheme.

Waverley departing Newcastle in 1981 on one of her few visits to the Tyne.

Waverley passing the Hawthorn Leslie shipyard at Walker-on-Tyne in 1981.

ten

The Forth

Above: Approaching Burntisland on a stormy day in 1982, when she poked her nose into the harbour, but the skipper decided not to call.

Right: Arriving at Granton in 1982. This slide had the authors puzzling over the location for a long time before it was recognised!

Opposite above: At Grangemouth in 1982, in the unkempt surroundings of a commercial dock in stormy conditions.

Opposite below: On *Waverley*'s second visit to the Forth in 1982, passing under the Forth Bridges.

Other titles published by Tempus

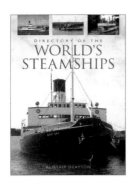

Directory of the World's Steamships
ALISTAIR DEAYTON

Steamships today are a dying breed and each year for the past half-century more and more have made their way to the breaker's yard. In his *Directory*, Alistair Deayton sets out to catalogue every operational passenger-carrying steamship and steamboat in existence. From the handful of surviving steam turbine-powered cruise ships down to tiny steam launches, this volume details a variety of vessels of all sizes and is a must for all steamship enthusiasts.
978 0 7524 4208 2

Caledonian Steam Packet Company Ltd
ALISTAIR DEAYTON

The Caledonian Steam packet Co. Ltd was formed in 1889 as the steamer-owning arm of the Caledonian Railway when the railway extended from Greenock to Gourock. In 1973 the company finally merged with David MacBrayne to form Caledonian MacBrayne. Illustrated with over 200 images of the ships of the fleet, the locations they served and the men who served on them, this book is an informative history of the company and its vessels from the 1880s to the persent day.

978 0 7524 2381 4

MacBrayne Steamers
ALISTAIR DEAYTON

For the past 150 years the name of MacBrayne has been synonymous with shipping in the West Highlands of Scotland. MacBraynes were so much a part of the scene in that there was a parody of the pslam *The earth is the Lord's, and all it contains, except the Western Isles, which belong to MacBraynes.* As well as providing tourist services, the MacBrayne steamers and ferries were, and still are, a vital lifeline for the islands of Scotland.

978 0 7524 2362 3

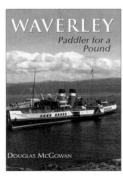

Waverley Paddler for a Pound
DOUGLAS MCGOWAN

Waverley, the world's last sea-going paddle steamer, was destined for the scrap yard in 1974 when Douglas McGowan and the Paddle Steamer Preservation Society purchased her for the princely sum of £1 and the rest is, as they say, history. Fresh from a £7 million refit in Great Yarmouth, *Waverley* is resplendent in her black, red and white livery and can be seen sailing the coast of Britain again.

978 0 7524 2877 2

If you are interested in purchasing other books published by Tempus, or in case you have difficulty finding any Tempus books in your local bookshop, you can also place orders directly through our website

www.tempus-publishing.com